LEAD YOUR SHIP

UNLOCK YOUR TRUE SELF AND CAPTAIN YOUR
SHIP LIKE A BOSS

SHIRLEY BAEZ

Print ISBN: 979-8-9877574-2-0

DEDICATION

This labor of love is in dedication to my biggest cheerleader, Aunt Carmen. My aunt has been with me through my ups, downs, breakdowns, and breakthroughs. She has been the voice of reason and the morning whispers telling me to believe in myself and not be afraid to take chances; what is for me has not yet been reached.

PREFACE

This book means so much to me because I am sharing stories of my evolution as leader and know that it will inspire others seeking greatness in their lives. When I came of age, I acknowledged the struggles I have faced in my life and the breakthroughs I have experienced. I knew that writing my story would be worthwhile for others fighting and trying to overcome challenges and adversities in life. Because I have always been very imaginative, I have always looked at things from a colorful aspect where I could to create my ideal outcomes, at least in my head.

From a young age, I wanted to be successful though the cards were stacked against me. That led me to think big and what it would look like to be on the other side of greatness. As a young adult, I was desperately trying to find an outlet that would allow me to flourish, be somebody, and get out of the darkness I found myself growing up in.

I found it my purpose to write this about something people can experience and read and know that there is light on the other end of the tunnel. I know that it was my duty to take the time to write this story because I am tired of seeing many girls lacking guidance and good role models to guide them and thus letting opportunities expire. I want to enlighten girls that have gone astray in a world where social media and what is socially acceptable rule. I want them to break those stigmas and walk in their shoes like the *bosses* they are.

I want to help young ladies that are lacking self-confidence, good role models, guidance, enlightenment, and perspective to see themselves as warriors, not as worriers, not as victims but as *victors*. I need to say that doing things scared provides a break-through and a sense of freedom within yourself. If you only get out of your head and believe in yourself, *dare* yourself!

Suppose I had someone give me those words of encouragement when I was young; I could have aimed for much bigger and more challenging goals, but I did not.

I sometimes ask myself, *What if?* of those times that I let prime opportunities pass by because I was apprehensive. I'm also glad that through tough times and being at the very bottom, I was able to grow like the lotus, the most beautiful flower growing from the mud. To experience growth and gain perspective and wisdom, you must go through the mud, obstacles, and sufferings of life.

CHAPTER 1
FIND YOUR SAIL

"You have no need to travel anywhere. Journey within yourself, enter a mine of rubies and bathe in the splendor of your own light."

RUMI

Why do intelligent, articulate, young women with great potential at success sometimes self-sabotage their hopes for better life opportunities?

Growing up in New York, I was adrift at sea, feeling lost, confused, and directionless. My dad and mom had gotten divorced; I did not have two parents to guide and encourage me. My dad worked many hours, so I only saw him every other week, and my mom was practically absent as she struggled with her gambling addiction. I had to grow up quickly, take care of myself, and go at it alone, not having somebody I could emulate to build the foundation of becoming a confident and successful young lady. I was lost at sea with ocean waters moving me about, not truly knowing myself and where I was going.

I struggled with finding my path and, most importantly, who I was. I got into abusive relationships, which further diminished my self-esteem. I was very creative and was involved in many activities that nourished those talents; however, I didn't have the role model I needed to encourage and cheer me on, providing me with guidance so I could keep pursuing what I loved. I dropped out of high school and was in an abusive relationship; that's when I hit rock bottom. I knew something was out there; I knew there was much more to life than what I was living.

I decided I needed to change so I went to register for college and see if I was eligible for a grant. My credentials were returned as unqualified for grants because my dad made too much money; even though I didn't live with him then. Feeling defeated, I walked back through the train station. There, I saw this big kiosk and sign saying, "We'll pay for your college." When I saw that, I knew that was my calling; I knew that was my sign. It happened to be a kiosk for the U.S. Army. That was precisely the calling I was looking for, and that's when I decided to join the United States Army. Around this time, terrorists struck the twin towers in downtown New York. At the same time, I made a vow that I would join the military and be committed to that path toward service.

I had gained my purpose at that moment; but I still didn't know where I was heading, what I was doing, where I was going, or what the outcome would be. A lot of these uncertainties play tricks in our minds, like witches trying to cast spells on our sanity and the massive decisions we make in our lives. Those were the same questions ruminating in my mind as I decided to change the course of my life. Although I was unhappy where I was in life before the military, it was still familiar territory. I couldn't shake off the feeling of wanting to pursue the path of higher learning and higher purpose but didn't know how to go about it. I needed to think creatively to achieve the right path in my life and start guiding myself toward a better future.

I know that for many young women living in a bustling city, not having a parent or good role model to support and encourage them can be challenging. Lacking support and still in the developing phase in their lives, they have no choice but to figure it out alone, to figure out who they are, want to do, and want to be when they grow up. You might see social media as your example of what good, perfect, or right should look like, which is far from the truth.

I challenge you to ask yourself if you are following your life's path or following somebody else's. Are you growing and leading yourself according to your values?

What are your values?

What's important to you?

How do you incorporate them into your daily life?

Who are the people you admire that share those same values?

What is the definition of *value*? In Webster's dictionary, it gives the meaning of values as "the things you believe are essential in how you live and work.".

Therefore making a conscious effort to identify your values is so important.

Values should determine your priorities as well as identify your gifts and purpose, enabling you to lead yourself and others.

As you drift through life trying to find these answers, you will realize the need to create a solid foundation to become the self-assured woman you are destined to be. Now more than ever, we must cultivate feelings of self-worth, acceptance, and love for ourselves.

In this book, we will look for ways to dig deep, finding truth and gratitude for ourselves and our lives. A new way forward means we can't hold on too tightly to our self-defeating thoughts as we create the life we want in our personal and professional lives. Through these self-leadership principles, you will discover the tools you need to sail through the sea of infinite possibilities.

This book contains keys to the answers you are searching for. Should you manifest what you read here, it has the power to change your life. As you read my life story, you will see that God, the Universe, or the entity you believe in, protects, and restores you as you take the necessary steps to finally break through. If you read this book and take action, it will change your life and shift you into a new dimension and higher levels of goal attainment. You will not be the only recipient of this shift; it will alter the trajectory of your lineage as well.

Take a moment and write down the answer to these questions.

Reflections:

1. Who are you?
2. Who would people say you are?
3. What are your values (non-negotiables)
4. What are some of your gifts and talents/strengths?
5. What are the principles you go by every day?

NOTES

CHAPTER 2
BUILD YOUR SAIL

"The woman who follows the crowd will usually go no further than the crowd. The woman who walks alone is likely to find herself in places no one has ever been before."

ALBERT EINSTEIN

As you go forward, you acknowledge you are made for much more. When I enlisted in the military, I didn't know what I was getting into. I didn't know what it entailed. I just knew that one, I wanted to serve my country after the events of September 11th and two, I wanted to go to college and get a higher education.

It was rough at first, but at least I had something to look forward to because I was so lost when I was in New York. There, I was in an abusive relationship with no parental guidance, that example that I needed; I had to figure it out on my own.

Still in the military, I was in an unknown realm, an unknown world. Not everybody enlisted in the military; I think it's about one of 1 percent of the population. I was the first in my family to enlist in the military. It was something new, not only for me but for everybody in my family; however, I knew deep inside that I needed to make a change.

I needed to do something with my life; there was something more in me, something that I needed to put out into the world. I didn't know what that was, all I knew was that I needed a change of scenery, a change of environment as a nineteen-year-old in a profession that requires full attention. After a lot of training, being in an ambiguous and dangerous environment, especially at that time after the tragedy of September 11th, I went into the military. I was getting prepared to deploy to an unknown environment where I didn't even know if I was going to come back, but I didn't even think about those things.

All I knew was that I needed to get out of New York, I needed a change, and I needed somewhere I belonged so I could grow. I didn't know if the military was that, but it was an escape. It was a gateway to change. I always knew that I had a lot to offer to myself and others. My sailboat was bare. It didn't have anything on it at first because again, it was adrift. My sails weren't fully developed. I was restricted and alone; I was in a new environment, I still had my sailboat, although the sails weren't fully developed. I needed to create and build them as I proceeded. In this new environment, I still had a lack of confidence, lack of direction, and was afraid of the unknown.

I didn't know what was required of me. But here I am and here I was, ready to move forward. For a lot of us, we know that we need to leave situations that do not fit us: that do not make us better people. We need to leave environments and situations that are little by little destroying our creativity, decrepitating us because we're not being exposed to an environment that provides us the opportunity to grow and be the best versions of ourselves. I know that a lot of you, especially young women that are lost and trying to find yourselves, fear what you may find, of what you can, or would encounter. I am telling you that what you find will be your motivation to make a shift once you realize you are made for more. You are here on this earth to grow, to explore the depths of your being, and creativity.

You're here to be an example for those you lead, for your community, and for yourself. Many times, as young women, we're placed under pressure. We put pressure on ourselves to be the best. We put pressure on ourselves to look a certain way, to dress a certain way, to speak a certain way, or to feel a certain way, so little by little, our identities diminish. If you start reflecting on who you truly want to be, and that's excluding what you see on TV or what you see on social media, you will find that there are a lot of environments out there for you to include yourself in, that will provide you the opportunity to start building your sailboat.

For me, that was the military. And I will tell you that whatever you choose as your environment; to explore what you're made of and what you can do is going to be scary. Everything unknown is scary, but as children, we imagine so much, and we don't even think about it. We imagine being all these things in life and we don't even think about it. We take bold steps, like a toddler, just walking in the middle of the street; maybe not knowing that there are going to be cars that might come along and hurt them.

Well, that might be an accident. They're just bold enough to follow what their imagination says and that is something we lose as we grow; as we get exposed to negative environments, we lose that.

I'm here to tell you you're not alone. You can build your boat little by little, building that sail to direct you to your ideal place, to your ideal destination, don't be scared. Everything always comes full circle. What are the things you are putting into play to build that sail? For me, it was taking chances, being, and taking chances in my life.

For me, being challenged was to be placed in situations during training that would challenge my critical thinking skills, that would have me negotiate myself and my team through an obstacle course that only as a team we would be able to negotiate, to go to the range and use my weapon to proficiently hit my target. It took a lot of practice, but I still went ahead and did it because there was a bigger purpose. Sometimes, we are put in situations where we have no choice but to excel because there is no other choice but to win. During that time however, I battled with self-esteem and self-confidence issues. I still didn't believe that I could be this great soldier that could shoot, and perfectly at that, that could run two miles under thirteen minutes, and that could go through an obstacle course unafraid, although I could have fallen and hurt myself.

I also had the challenge of being in a male-dominated environment where they also looked at females as maybe weaker or in need of help in certain things. I didn't want help. I wanted enlightenment. I wanted to find myself and I needed to do that from within, little by little. What I built were the sails that would have my boat to sail into unforeseen territories, as I was challenged to study and understand the language of the military; and how to lead, not only myself but lead others. You know, you're not going to know where you're going if you don't take the time to know yourself.

You're not going to know where that boat is going to be headed, but you have to give yourself that opportunity to find that out, to understand more about yourself, to know and challenge yourself. It is when you conquer yourself and stretch that it starts making sense. That's when it becomes clear to you that you are strong from within, that maybe there's something here.

That is when you can overcome those challenges that you were once afraid to confront because you are now getting to know yourself and thus stronger; the fear is subsiding little by little. As you go through the perils of life, you see that when you come upon an obstacle, you look at it, you negotiate it and go through it as you're still evaluating yourself and the choices you make thus making the obstacle that much easier to overcome.

You now feel so proud of yourself because you didn't even think about your internal barriers. You're not even thinking about your internal fears and your sadness. You're now thinking about the actions you I will take and the resources you will use to overcome doubt and breakthrough because you know that's what's going to make you a better person at the end.

As I went through each of these obstacles, little by little, I built my sails and thus, bit by bit, built my sailboat. The sail was coming along, coming together as it was directing me, and I was directing it to where I wanted to go, which I still didn't know a hundred percent. As I crossed each obstacle, I felt better and better.

By practicing your courage every day, you will start building yourself and building that character, that strong woman that you know you are, into a complete warrior. Still, I tried and tried, and I kept trying, but there were more obstacles that I needed to negotiate as well as delve from within to figure out who I was, who I was becoming, and who I needed to be for myself and everybody else.

Reflections:

1. What are your fears?
2. What steps can you take to overcome them?
3. What are your superpowers?
4. Where would you be if fear weren't a factor?

NOTES

CHAPTER 3
YOU THROUGH THE LOOKING GLASS; BUILDING YOUR TELESCOPE

"Self-reflection is necessary to dig beneath our own layers and visit the inner crevices of our heart and mind to develop an understanding of life."

UNKNOWN

Now that I was in the military and could get away from my previous life, that was not going to get me anywhere. I started finding unusual strengths because I never challenged myself until I came into the service. The service stretched me; put me in a position to see how far I could go, see what I could accomplish, and be exposed to people that would change my life and influence me in different ways. That changed me as a soldier, as a woman, and now, as a leader. Still, as a young soldier coming off from the streets of New York, it was still hard for me to get a grip on finding myself and finding where I was going with this new life. It was hard. These were also roadblocks as to how quickly I was going to be successful.

When we feel lost, it's hard for us to solidify who we are, and own up to know our strengths because we're still lacking that self-confidence. However, I was still in a new environment that offered me the opportunity to stretch myself, but that didn't come without much self-reflection.

I remember when I felt very down as a young soldier and was thinking about why I was getting pushback from my colleagues. Or why wasn't I getting ahead fast enough? Was it that people were against me; was it that victimhood mentality that I still had from being in New York, from always feeling that I never had an opportunity because of circumstances?

I had to sit down and think about that and then it just clicked. I started thinking that I'm being exposed to these opportunities, although they are challenging and hard. I'm starting to see myself in a little bit of a new light because I'm doing things, I never thought about doing before.

Then it clicked in my head that maybe it wasn't the external environment, maybe it wasn't other people, but maybe it was within me because I still brought back the self-limiting beliefs that I had inside due to the environment I came from. I needed to take time, reexamine myself from within so I could have a solid direction of where I wanted to go in this new life. I needed to build my telescope. Telescopes are very important because they will guide you in the right direction. You can see through them and have a clearer picture of where you're going, but that doesn't come without self-improvement

Many times, self-confidence comes from self-limiting beliefs stemming from childhood, it makes you scared to be great, you're scared to grow, and you're scared of who you might become. You may end up being a successful person, something you dreamed about before. I didn't have the opportunity or the courage to pursue that, to pursue that person, or to pursue that direction. One powerful principle I took upon was reflecting through journaling. I became enamored with buying notebooks and writing my thoughts of how I felt, what I did that day, how it made me feel, and how I could improve.

What were some of the things that I did right in my eyes and some of the things that, again, I needed to improve? And those helped me a lot because I would go back to them. I would stop writing, leave it for a couple of days, then come back and read it and see the improvement.

I took the time to sit down and have a retrospective approach to my week; things that bothered me, things that made me cry, and things that made me sad. During that time, it was a mixture of things, a mixture of the old and the new; the old being, the environment that I came from and the new environment, which stretched me and challenged me.

That was painful because although it was more painful to be in my old environment, it was something I knew and was already familiar with, but still, I had to look from within and only I could do that. Now, what I loved about this new environment was that I found a tribe of people that were like-minded like me, that were striving to stretch themselves too. That helped me so much in the support I needed to keep forging forward.

Aside from looking from within, through journaling, through self-reflection, find those people that will support you and are also walking that same path and together, build that telescope where it's going to lead you in the right direction. You need to do things in life that are probably not popular or enticing; they're going to be hard, but you need to find yourself to know where you're going.

It is hard to find yourself, especially as you develop as a leader, especially if you are a young, professional woman with ambitions, dreams, and aspirations, of being great, of being seen, of being known, of being acknowledged, whereas before, maybe not so much. You were not accepted; you have to take the hardships, right? Most importantly, you have to know where you're going. I challenge you to look from within, to take time, to sit, to reflect, to journal your thoughts, your feelings, your plan, and your lessons learned; put down the notebook and then come back to it a couple of days or a couple of weeks later to see what has changed.

You'll see what a problem is still, what needs improvement, as well as what has improved. The areas that you've been successful at, own it, little by little, own it; give yourself those small victories. I know it's going to be hard because we are coming from the shadows, we are our worst critiques, but if we want to be seen and heard; you must dare to believe in yourself and own your successes instead of downplaying them. In this way, you are owning your voice and gaining control better steer that Sailboat toward your destiny.

Reflections:

1. What is stopping you from owning your superpowers?
2. How can you authentically show up for yourself and others?
3. What have you learned about yourself that you was not aware of before?

NOTES

CHAPTER 4
OWNING YOUR POWERS

The power of owning our stories, even the difficult ones, is that we get to write the ending.

BRENE BROWN

After taking some needed time for reflection during a confusing time in my life when I didn't know my place in the military. I started realizing that I had this feeling of taking ownership of my path and thus, my powers. I needed to self-reflect to build that telescope, to orient me, and show me how to be successful in my military career, but I needed to do the work. There were a lot of days and nights that I reflected. It was intentional observing my strengths and weaknesses to understand why things were happening to me and why things were not working for me in my professional life. I realized I could re-frame my thoughts to being a victor instead of a victim. When I began switching my studies, I started gaining power and strength within myself, which was reflected in my approach to projects, environments, people, etc., which I then remembered in the outcome of my work.

I started realizing that maybe I'm not a victim of circumstances, not now, and not before. I can use my power, creative gifts, and desire to serve as a creator, do productive work, give back, and succeed. You have so much more to give to the world. Still, for whatever reason, we live behind our shadows because we are afraid of being judged and we feel as though if we are successful, we are afraid that people will find out that we are false, hence, feeling of impostor syndrome. We need to own the powers that we shine through. It was hard for me to see my successes and I felt that others didn't either, but that was because I didn't see it in myself first.

I played small the whole time until I reflected and took ownership of the areas I needed to improve. When I did this, people started seeing that I was serious about who I was and what I wanted to do. That came through the adjustment of my telescope by reflection, understanding who I was, and my purpose and dedication to learning and studying. This gave me the tools to own up to my successes and failures through tangible and intangible means. It was also important for me to humble myself and ask for help from my mentors who provided a good perspective, outside looking in. My mentors were my cheerleaders, so I did not feel alone on my sailboat because I saw individuals ready to support and help me; they always believed in me more than I believed in myself.

I started gravitating toward my powers and attaining confidence because of my leadership subordinates. Now they were looking to me for leadership and guidance, to mold them into the leaders they wished to become. When I started tapping into my powers, everything around me began to shift to my benefit. Everybody began to respond differently; the work I was doing was more polished, clear, and tangible for others to follow. If we do the work and listen with a humble heart to others whom we look up to, we will see the return on investment soon enough. We have so much to provide to the world, let's pick up that baton and lead the way by first leading ourselves.

We must show up and show out. We are powerful and audacious women, the queens of our thrones. We must embrace our gifts and talents; we can tackle anything. We need to be honest with our own internal struggles so that we can feel secure in our skin, which only sheds when leveling up. Once I began knowing my powers and providing my gifts to the world, I started to scale up the ranks. People then saw me for leadership, coaching, and being an inspiration in their lives. I knew then that I had the responsibility of being and becoming the best I could be, not only for me but for others.

With that, I was more self-aware, cognizant of what I was doing, and through my initiation of lifelong self-development, self-care, and self-love I could lead myself healthily. I wasn't afraid to take charge, speak in public, voice my opinion for fear of not being liked or judged, or make decisions about what was best for my soldiers and the organization. I didn't come to that point haphazardly; I had to do the work and toil through my internal demons and feelings of inadequacy because of abandonment issues so that I could shed that dead skin and forge forward toward new horizons.

As I went through this journey, I started coming across other women who exhibited the same characteristics as I did when I had self-doubt, lacked confidence, and played small. It was easy to recognize because they represented the old me and I knew I had to do something about that. Now it was my responsibility to help them break through precisely what I had gone through. That filled my cup because I was changing lives for the better so that I could develop them into future leaders and not be afraid to lead like the bosses they were meant to be. I wanted to teach this through the principles of leadership and self-leadership so that they could *lead their ship*.

That all came about when I was owning and becoming the leader and woman that I was truly meant to be that guided me to lead authentically. Remember, you can hide your insecurities from everyone else, but you can't hide it from yourself because if you do, you are then lying to others, and it will reflect in the end. When you fail at something, look at it as an opportunity, not a failure; we should all fail forward. Know your strengths and manage your weaknesses, analyze your setbacks, and improve them as it will make you more strategic about your life and leading others.

Adjust your telescope, clean it up through self-reflection, know yourself and understand yourself so that you can own your powers and abilities to be the leader in your personal and professional life. Remember that the most important thing is to see ourselves as victors, not victims. We now have a more substantial anchor, stronger sails, and a cleaner telescope showing us what's on the horizon. Now you are sailing toward you and success.

Reflections:

1. What have you learned through your falls?
2. What resources do you use to better yourself and your abilities?
3. What is your Self-love/ Self-are routine
4. What steps can you take to have grace for yourself when things don't go as planned?

NOTES

CHAPTER 5
LEAD YOUR SHIP

"Our deepest fear is not that we are inadequate. Our deepest fear is that we are powerful beyond measure."

MARIANNE WILLIAMSON

Now that you understand yourself and have taken ownership of your strength and weaknesses; now that you see yourself as a victor and not a victim; now you're starting to own up to your circumstances. You now own your circumstances and understand the depth of your powers towards a situation so that you can take the proper action.

At the beginning, I was so afraid to be the lead on anything. I always hid in the back, praying. This is while I was in a military mind you. I prayed that nobody called me up to participate or be the leader in something because I was so afraid to look stupid. That's what I thought, at least, because subconsciously, I always thought that people didn't care to know my thoughts; that people thought I was a joke, that people didn't even care about what I had to say, or that I even had anything relevant to provide. Those were the thoughts that went through my head without even knowing what people thought, but I felt it. This was also a byproduct of how I felt about myself and my abilities. I used to pray that I wouldn't be selected to speak in front of a group; that I wasn't asked for my opinion because I didn't understand what I could bring to the table.

I decided to sit at the table and even own the table. I know a lot of you choose to hide in the back because you think that your thoughts and ideas are irrelevant to the group, which is so erroneous. For that reason, I've missed out on so many opportunities. I still think about it today. I still fight against that today. That imposter syndrome, not living up to my true self, to my true potential because I, myself didn't believe that I could be that great. How then could anybody else believe it? This is absurd but we must take responsibility and take over what our minds, our survival instincts are trying to tell us so that we don't stretch ourselves.

Don't get me wrong, our minds are not telling us this because we don't want the best for ourselves. We just want to survive. We just want to feel comfortable. When you are in your comfort zone is where you least grow, when you are in your comfort, you hide yourself from potential a sea of options that can open to a lot of great and unique experiences and opportunities. Once I understood this, I was able to stretch and grow. These were baby steps, and environment had a lot to do with it. The military environment did stretch me. There were many times where I didn't have any choice. Maybe you too need to reach a point where you have no other choice.

Luckily, many of you don't have a choice but to be comfortable with being uncomfortable. To stretch yourself by placing yourself and embracing the discomfort of being in that specific situation.

Whether making massive decisions to take massive action in your personal and professional life, you need to challenge yourself to take the lead, in a group, on a project, or in a situation. You can't live your life hiding in the shadows because you are diminishing yourself to what you can offer others. And that is something I had to learn for myself, that others could benefit from my leadership.

Once I started understanding my powers, I was unafraid to speak up, ask for what I wanted, and provide my opinions on different matters. I was unafraid to make people or my superiors mad; I was confident. Now, those things have pros and cons because while some of my supervisors saw that as being audacious and self-confident, others saw it as a potential threat, disrespect, or how dare you. But I meant it with great intentionality because I was trying to care for myself and others. I was looking for my career path, which I had every right to do. When I was leading others and looking out for my group's interest as their leader, my group looked up to me because I protected them.

But now that you understand your skills and abilities, you can take charge of your life. You can make decisions in your life that will enhance its quality, whether investing correctly or purchasing something that will increase in value or bring you a rate of return. You may even be entertaining the idea of becoming an entrepreneur. For example, suppose you are a mom with an idea you want to launch and thus make your kid's life better or ask for what you deserve through negotiating a pay raise or in the workplace, not being afraid to take on projects that you otherwise would not. In that case, you now dare to create what you want and live the life you always imagined without fear to go after it. You can't live life scared anymore.

What I've learned throughout my experience in my professional led me to be less afraid to make decisions and act. Of course, I had to make decisions for the mission's success in the environment I was operating in. But you still have to make decisions in life because you'll see yourself in settings where decisions and decisive action need to take place.

But I think that even when you're not in a combat zone, you should not be afraid to make workplace decisions. Look at it as your mini combat mission, where you are trying to survive, and surviving means using your powers, your ownership of your strengths, and making decisions that will benefit you. Try to correlate that also to benefit the organization. That is a win-win in your professional life, but you must let yourself be seen and heard. Believe that you can accomplish what you think is impossible and be intentional about it.

You can't look at something and automatically discard it because you think you're not the right person to do it. Yes, you are the right person to do it. And that's why it's so important that you are fearless as you get ready to forge forward. Don't even think about it; just commit to doing it. You'll see that you'll be leading your ship.

You must be the owner of your life and destiny by taking leadership of your personal and professional life—no more hiding. There was a time when I was leading.

Some of my soldiers were top-notch. I already knew many of them knew more than I did in some areas of our work, and I was their leader. I'm not going to deny it; that did intimidate me at first because I thought they would think I was an idiot, or they would not respect me because I didn't know as much as them, or they were not going to take me seriously.

Yes, there was a time when they were not taking me seriously, and it wasn't because I didn't necessarily know a particular subject. Because of my self-consciousness and low self-esteem, I was projecting into the environment. My Soldiers could smell it, see it, and feel it. That's why there were times at first when I was weak in that area. As a result, I was afraid to get out of my office. I was so afraid to interact with them and ask them how they were feeling and how their families and kids were, and it showed through their demeanor towards me; it was a horrible time. Leaders should always want to know what their troops are doing in their personal and professional lives.

Even if you're not a leader, that's what you need to do with the people that you work with so that you can get to know them better, build a rapport, and strengthen bonds. That's why they didn't take me seriously at first because they didn't think that I was taking them seriously or taking the mission seriously. After all, I was so engulfed in my little victimhood mentality and thought that I wasn't good enough to be worthy of that position. I was given that position for a reason and I needed to own up to that. There were times when yes, I was leading my team and I felt a little concerned that I would not make the right decision, or they might think that it was the wrong decision because I thought that I didn't know what I needed to know, but you're never going to know what you need to know all the time.

You just have to kind of look at the situation and make the most informed decision with the information you have at the time and make it with full force confidence, and that's what I did. You know, there was a point when I said enough is enough. It's going to be me versus me. This point came about one day when I was having coffee with a colleague, I trusted who worked within the same organization, providing insights into how some of my Soldiers felt towards me.

He acknowledged that my Soldiers lost confidence in me and my leadership; they knew I was competent but lacked the confidence. Shoot, I even had one Soldier try to sabotage to get me fired by gathering all the troops without my permission to talk behind my back and vote on how to do so. Why would my team/ Soldiers feel this way about it? I started contemplating and thinking back to the days when 1. I was afraid to engage with my Soldiers 2. Not taking an interest in knowing how they and their families were doing because I was too shy to engage 3. lacked clear guidance when there was a task because I was worried, they wouldn't abide or give me grief as to why; 3—scared of being judged. Can you believe that? So, I was always vague and left it to them to decide, very unbecoming of a leader.

The news broke me down to my core; I felt my heart palpating, bleeding like a wound for which there was no medicine, bandage, or cure. But, at the same time, I was so angry with myself for letting this go for so long. I genuinely loved and cared for my Soldiers, so at that moment, I knew that something needed to change and that something was me going inward and facing my self-limiting beliefs.

I asked my boss for a couple of days off in which I then retreated to my magical place, the beach, as I sat on the balcony of my hotel room overlooking the Sunset. I felt the wind in my face as I watched the waves wash up the beach and into the ocean. I reminded myself that if I was entrusted with this unique position, I needed to go back into my treasure chest, retrieve my crown, put it back on my head where it belonged, and own this opportunity, not only for me but for the ones I loved and led. Everything after that revelation changed forever!

I came back from that weekend with a clear understanding of what I needed to do. I started engaging in all aspects of my organization, from overcoming my shyness and engaging my Soldiers with intention to making hard and unpopular decisions with confidence. I ensured that in the areas where I was weak, I empowered those that were strong without feeling threatened. I was a leader who was open to listening to others' perspectives and opinions but understanding that it was up to me to make the final call. I started building an environment of trust and empowerment, becoming a servant leader, and leading my ship.

When you are in a group of individuals of high caliber, it's understandable to feel uneasy or unsure about your abilities and worthiness as a leader. You must discard those thoughts; think about the mission you are tasked to accomplish and know where your powers lie —believing in yourself and feeling confident in your skin. Take action in your professional life so you can scale, climb the ladder, and open yourself to unbelievable opportunities.

Stop playing small. Your only job in life is not just to wake up and go to work, take care of the kids and do it again. You're much more than that. You can expand and lead yourself into more prominent roles or other opportunities outside of your professional life, such as growing your wealth hence your legacy to leave your kids or your family. You know, there's power in taking action, and that's through self-leadership. You are going to benefit. And the people around you will benefit just as much.

Reflection:

1. What internal fears are blocking from leading?
2. How can you communicate authentically to those you serve?
3. What areas in your environment do you need to change to take action now?

NOTES

CHAPTER 6
LEVELING UP

"Success doesn't come from what you do occasionally,
it comes from what you do consistently."

MARIE FORLEO

We now dare to take action because of the tools collected to build our sailboat. We can now sail into clear waters, reflecting on our period of drifting in the sea of nothingness, of being lost and lonely. We began building our sails; they were a little weak at first but have gotten firmer and more robust because we knew we wanted something better for our lives.

We've collected our telescope to give us a better preview of where we are going. If we were arriving at an island or solid structure through self-examination, we reflect that it looked clear in the distance and thus can plan for our arrival and what we will do once we arrive. As it looked clear, we understood who we were and who we were meant to be. We started walking fearlessly towards the world less traveled. We don't know our final destination, but we know there is much to do in this infinite sea called life. We now understand our strengths and manage our weaknesses, thus owning the powers that enable us to proceed with our goals in our lives, careers, and happiness through the value we bring to others and the world.

Now it's time to level up because we've collected and been crafting quite a bit. It's simple; the tools we've collected along the way made our sails a little thicker and easier to control throughout our path. This enables us to maneuver our sailboat with more precision and efficiency. Our telescope, as I said before, is precise. In the end, the vision is clear.

We understand how we are. We know our compass, which is another essential tool in our sailboat. As we sail through the seas, we know our compass through our values. Understanding our values is vital for our compass to point us in the right direction of who we are and what makes us happy, fulfilled, and confident.

Constant self-development, constant intentionality of our growth, reflection of ourselves, and meditation will help us level up. This is what the Greek philosophers often did. That's why they had so much wisdom. I love Greek philosophy because it goes in-depth into our souls to understand our potential and who we are as humans.

Constantly ask yourself, what is my purpose? That question is critical to contemplate as an evolving woman and an integral part of this world. You need to exercise this daily to understand what you are made here to accomplish. To continuously level up means having the right mentors and the right group of people with similar goals and mindsets will encourage and challenge you to improve. They can walk that path less traveled with you, so you won't get discouraged. We need people who can emotionally feed us positivity when feeling worthless or lacking self-esteem.

You can't be around other people that weigh you down or are not at the same level of growth that you are at. You're both going to shrivel up into nothingness. You need to be around people who dare to take risks and take massive action, have the confidence to be comfortable in their skin, and not care what other people think. That's what I started doing toward the latter part of my military career. Once I began to transition, I began building my tribe because of my transition out of the military.

We all go through life changes, but I think the point here is that no matter what end of a shift or energy you are at in your life, you need to surround yourself with like-minded individuals that can meet you at your level. Those are the people you need maintain by your side.

These people will help you navigate the rough waters of self-doubt, the turbulent waters of indecisions about approaches you take in your personal and professional life. What helped build my tribe was networking, putting myself out there, getting outside my shell and speaking with people, getting to know them, and caring to hear their stories. As I said in earlier chapters, I was afraid for people to talk to me and scared for people to pick on me or listen to my opinion or ideas. I was so self-conscious, even unsure of anything I did or said.

Once intentional about your success and well-being, you've learned to love yourself and only want the best for yourself. You are exerting that power within you and owning it 100 percent. When you acknowledge that, the sky's the limit because you'll always want to be better. You'll always want to learn more and be curious about new discoveries. You'll always want more out of life because you know that living a basic life is no longer an option.

Leveling up for me means constant self-development, volunteering, knowing when to ask for help, and being accountable for what goes right and wrong. An example of this would be volunteering for a job that no one else wants to do because that will also provide opportunities for breakthroughs. That's also going to make you be seen. But what's going to help you the most is being around people you know are making strides in their careers and lives

As you are evolving, you must always, always, always keep your survival instincts at bay as it will sike to wanting to play small or stay in a safe place. We'll always have to strive to stretch ourselves. For some reason, stretching my mind is something I battle daily. I always snap out of it, though. I then reflect on it, write about it, speak about it, reflect on it, and then I move forward confidently in life.

Understanding that there will be times when you need help is vital to your success. It's hard to ask for help because we think we are perceived as weak; it is the total opposite. Humble yourself and ask for help from a friend, a colleague, or maybe a mentor to build fresh ideas and perspective or even to get you out of a rut. You are here to render your gifts to the world.

That is when you are truly going to live in fulfillment. You'll feel confident about yourself because there's nothing more significant than giving back and contributing to somebody else's growth, success, and evolution. You are the queen of your throne. You are the queen of the sea. If you've had that crown sitting on a shelf for quite some time, it's time to reclaim it and place it in your head where it belongs.

Reflection:

1. What activities are you doing to help you level up?
2. What does success look like for you?
3. Who does your tribe consist of?
4. What do you want to render to the world?

NOTES

CHAPTER 7
JOURNEY TOWARD YOUR PURPOSE

"She was powerful not because she wasn't scared but because she went on so strongly, despite the fear."

ATTICUS

Your purpose should be to pour and be of value to others. When I was growing up, I was just in survival mode. I only thought about myself and how I would make it another day.

In the military, I was also in survival mode. I was still unsure who I was. When I took the time to do the internal work, I figured a lot of these out and dug deep into understanding why I felt like this. I was able to flourish. When I advanced, I grew as a leader and provided others with the resources needed to grow as leaders. The thing that opened my eyes was being exposed to myself through the eyes of the people I led.

If you are a professional woman leading others, trust me, your insecurities and all the baggage you bring will reflect if you don't get a handle on your insecurities and begin owning your powers.

I realized that I was affecting the people I cared most about, my soldiers. I paid a high price for that because I was leading them selfishly. It was about me and how I felt, how I was being perceived, and how competent I looked; it was all in my head, and thus my issues permeated out of me.

A leader is not just someone that people follow; a leader is someone that empowers and gains the trust and confidence of others who are allowing you to lead them. It's about the influence that you have on others through relationship building. Once you show that you care and that you're allowing them the opportunity to grow by empowering them, then trust fosters. When I started being intentional about serving my soldiers, truly grew as a person and a conscious leader. That's where I genuinely gained success.

Along the way, I made many mistakes, but I'm OK with making those mistakes because they led me to grow even more.

It's all about pouring into the benefit of your group and empowering them. You are training them, influencing them to be the next generation of leaders. When you have figured out the art of self-leadership, you will see that you will lead intentionally, reflecting on your environment. You must embrace the journey. Be confident that your sailboat is strong and that it's going to lead you to your path. Once you get enlightened by getting better, you can give back to others in a very healthy, clean, and compassionate way.

It is time to enjoy the journey toward your path and purpose. Now that you know yourself better and how you want to render those gifts, you've gained a sense of who you are; you are equipped to handle challenges and adversities that come your way. You are sure of yourself; you now place boundaries by the power of saying no. In my professional life, I didn't quite understand my boundaries, 99 percent of the time, I said yes because I didn't want to be seen as difficult or going against the grain. I feared not being liked or accepted in an all-male-dominated environment. I did not understand that I was saying no to myself by trying to please everyone, bringing exhaustion, resentment, and unhappiness to my life.

As you gain clarity about yourself your boundaries, and abilities, you are acquiring the necessary tools to build a sturdy sailboat as it was once adrift so that you can find self-empowerment and lead it toward your purpose. You began building yourself through reflection and knowing yourself, building character, and with that understanding, who you are inside and out. Once you know who you are, you can lead yourself and others better.

When you lean into your powers, purpose, and faith, you embrace failure easier because you see it as lessons learned. To lead your ship is to fail forward but be confident that you've gained the knowledge to steer your ship correctly, and your telescope will provide a comprehensive view of what's in the distant and near future; what to prepare for. Your compass will lead you to your true north; here is where the tools you've been gathering will help you build a sturdy and stable vehicle to steer it toward your objectives.

You want to be the leader of your life, your community, your department, or your section in your professional life. Be committed to doing the work within.

Extraordinary leaders, especially women, do the hard work. They must acknowledge all the ugliness, insecurities, and negativity we tell ourselves or let society tell us. When we discover ourselves, those extra things don't even matter. You know what you bring to the table. You know yourself well enough to defend yourself and your convictions. If anybody wants to tell you otherwise, you know how to stand up for yourself and, thus, stand for others.

The whole point here is to be self-directed by knowing yourself, your values, strengths, personality, talents, skills, and passions to live with purpose and intent. The goal is to be self-led, to love yourself, embrace yourself, embrace adversity, and see it as a stepping-stone to more significant opportunities.

There's no such thing as setbacks, only lessons learned. But enough of all that because you've heard all of this throughout the other chapters. Now it's time to be confident in your skin as you sail to your grand purpose. What is your purpose? One of your biggest purposes should be to pour into others and to give back because you know that within you lies a person that went through the school of hard knocks and came out resilient on the other side. All the toxicity and baggage you carried for so long can now be thrown off that sailboat, making it lighter to navigate more smoothly into your destiny. Now it's time to reclaim your crown. Are you prepared to wear it loudly and proudly? Lead like the queen you were always meant to be!

1. What are you doing in the service of others?
2. How would you lead yourself moving forward and others?
3. What are you willing to struggle for to find your purpose?
4. What do you want your legacy to be like?

NOTES

ABOUT THE
AUTHOR PAGE

Shirley Baez is the founder and CEO of the LeadHERship Academy, a company that empowers women to step into their power and captain their professional and personal lives as true bosses. Shirley is an inspirational force mentoring and coaching hundreds to find their true greatness.

She is a speaker and published author contributing to the book "POWERFUL FEMALE IMMIGRANTS WHO INSPIRE GREATNESS: 24 Women 24 Stories 24 Movements" where she tells her story of struggles to triumphs.

With 20-Years of military service in the Army Special Operations community and the recipient of multiple military achievement and recognition awards. Shirley now pursues her passion for helping people through her coaching, where she provides the tools, you need to lead your ship and succeed in your personal and professional life.

ACKNOWLEDGMENTS

Writing a book is no easy task but oh so worth it and rewarding. None of this would have been possible without the support of my aunt, Carmen Emenegildo. She's always been the voice of reason and the light that keeps showing me the way. She is not only my aunt but my best friend.

To my Dad, Rafael L. Baez, and my Stepmother, Maria Estela Debran de Baez, for always encouraging and believing in me. Their values and the integrity they lived by were the examples I needed growing up. Because although I couldn't understand it when I was young, I know now that it shaped me into the person I am.

I want to thank my Mother, Marianela A. Diplan. My upbringing wasn't easy, but it was what I needed. Living the "hard knock life" showed me resilience, grit, perseverance, and the power of imagination and hope. This time in my life gave me the tools to learn how to survive life and write a book about it.

Writing a book about the story of your life and how to inspire others is a surreal process. I'm forever indebted to Eli Gonzalez and The Ghost Publishing Company for your mentorship and challenge in writing a book in 60 days! I am grateful to Andrea Legato for her editorial help, keen insight, and ongoing support in bringing my story to life. Because of their efforts and encouragement, I have a legacy to pass on to my family, where one didn't exist before.

A special thanks to my beloved U.S. Army; and organization who brought me from the streets as a naïve Private and allowed me to grow and flourish. My time in the Military was unforgettable as I was stretched to be the best I could and to rise through the ranks to become a high-ranking female in one of the most elite communities; The Special Operations Forces community. I will never forget the Camaraderie, Brother, and Sisterhood I found there; it will forever be life-changing.

www.ingramcontent.com/pod-product-compliance
Lightning Source LLC
Chambersburg PA
CBHW060355130626
46553CB00003B/1246